Sustainable Design Solutions from the Pacific Northwest

SUSTAINABLE DESIGN SOLUTIONS FROM THE PACIFIC NORTHWEST
Vikram Prakash, series editor

Architects of the Pacific Northwest have been celebrated for a longstanding respect for the environment and a holistic view of our place in it. This series spotlights innovative design achievements by contemporary Northwest architects whose work reinforces core principles and ethics of sustainable design. Reflecting cross-disciplinary inspirations ranging from environmental sciences to sociology and systems biology, the pioneering buildings and technologies profiled in this series share common aesthetic and social goals. Promoting maximum energy efficiency through extensive use of recycled materials and minimal dependence on mechanical systems for heat, ventilation and waste management, these works demonstrate a profound and enduring love of the natural world and its ecological systems.

Studio at Large: Architecture in Service of Global Communities
by Sergio Palleroni, with Christina Eichbaum Merkelbach

Studio at Large

Architecture in Service of Global Communities

by Sergio Palleroni, in collaboration with Christina Eichbaum Merkelbach

UNIVERSITY OF WASHINGTON PRESS

Seattle and London

12/07

Studio at Large is published with the assistance of a grant from the University of Washington Architecture Publications Fund. It is also generously supported by a gift from Collier C. Kimball.

University of Washington Press
P.O. Box 50096, Seattle, WA 98145, U.S.A.
www.washington.edu/uwpress

Library of Congress Cataloging-in-Publication Data

Palleroni, Sergio. Studio-at-large : architecture in service of global communities / by Sergio Palleroni, in collaboration with Christina Eichbaum Merkelbach.—1st ed. p. cm.—(Sustainable design solutions from the Pacific Northwest) ISBN 0-295-98432-5 (pbk. : alk. paper)
1. Architecture—Study and teaching—Northwest, Pacific. 2. Building—Study and teaching—Northwest, Pacific. 3. Sustainable architecture. 4. Architects and community. 5. University of Washington. I. Merkelbach, Christina Eichbaum. II. Title. III. Series.
NA2005.P35   2004
728'.047'0711795—dc22   2004005931

The paper used in this publication is acid-free and recycled from 20 percent post-consumer and at least 50 percent pre-consumer waste. It meets the minimum requirements of American National Standard for Information Sciences—Permanence of Paper for Printed Library Materials, ANSI Z39.48-1984.

Design and composition by Christina Eichbaum Merkelbach

Front matter illustrations: *p. vi*, Juan Maria Morelos Elementary School Solar Kitchen in Colonia San Jose, Morelos, Mexico; *p. viii*, a typical cluster of homes in Colonia San Lucas, Morelos, Mexico (photo by Owen Gump); *p. xiv*, GCS Professor Jim Adamson takes *siesta* in Havana, Cuba (photo by Jeff Speert).

To my children
Ali, Nico, and Silvia
and all the children I have been blessed to know through these projects

Contents

School is so insulated, and architects have this jargon—it becomes a game of speaking in clever ways to explain your design. It's really nice to get out in the community and see real-life issues and problems and how architecture and good design can play a part in addressing them—but just a part. When you participate in a project like this, you can appreciate that design is important, good construction is important, but so is being sensitive and open. It's common sense. There's no magic thing you do. Students learn that they aren't heroes, that they're part of a continuum of hardworking activists.

Leslie Morishita
Housing and Community Planner,
Inter*Im Community Development Association

Introduction

A colorín tree stands as the lone impediment to the building of three classrooms of a primary school for children of the CIVAC squatter community Tescal, who have no other place to learn. The tree's bright scarlet flowers and seeds are harvested for dyes and traditional winter food; some make necklaces with them, and some add them to peanut tamales or fry them to mix with scrambled eggs. To save the tree would set an example in the community against deforestation and for the preservation of local sustainable resources. To remove it could save thousands of scarce dollars better spent on completing the building.

The fate of this tree had to be decided upon by thirty students near the end of their formal architectural education, many of whom were working in a group for the first time. In our design/build studios, when we make the decision to build, the issues at stake are not just aesthetic. Building engages the larger fabric of people's lives in ways that are complex and often contradictory. Issues of cultural heritage and sustainability often come into conflict with the realities of economic survival.

The dilemma of the colorín tree exemplifies the real-world situational learning absorbed by our students, who

The U.S. Pavilion in Auroville, Tamil Nadu, India. Photo by Pino Marchese.

are removed from their own familiar culture and forced to address unfamiliar issues while helping to create a building that belongs to the community. During the typically eleven-week programs, students discover the potential of the group's collective knowledge.

The students in 1996 chose to cut down the tree. In the end, pragmatic considerations prevailed. One student had calculated that saving the tree would have cost thirty children per year possibly their only avenue to escape severe poverty. On another day, facing different parameters, the solution might have been to save the tree. In the end, for the pedagogical process, deliberation and engagement with the complex issues at work were more important than the specific outcome.

Reestablishing the Relevance of Architecture Education

For many decades, architectural educators and practitioners have observed with increasing alarm the decline in significance of architectural work. Especially acute is the diminishment of architecture's power for social and cultural transformation . . . . Our profession, verging on irrelevance, has reached a critical juncture. Architecture schools must move quickly to respond seriously to the complexity of divergent and varied social demands.

Frances Bronet

Students gather around a colorín tree for a symbolic groundbreaking at the first Design/ Build Mexico program in 1995.

This and many similar critiques of architecture and architecture education have resounded through our profession in recent decades. In the *Princeton Report* (1968), Robert Geddes criticized higher education for being too disengaged from service to the community. In the early 1990s, other educators such as Thomas Dutton introduced concepts of critical pedagogy and ethnography into the discourse on architecture education. Many called for a reexamination of the social aspects of architectural practice and criticized architectural institutions for ignoring the potential of social activism in the field.

In 1996 the Carnegie Foundation for the Advancement of Teaching published a major study of architecture education, citing recommendations and goals for future reform. In this study, Ernest Boyer concludes: "Architects are too rarely admitted to the higher levels of decision-making in our society."[1] He

On the wall of a local tortilla shop, students charrette with the community.

further suggests that "schools of architecture could do more...to instill in students a commitment to lives of engagement and service."[2] Two questions haunt the impassioned call to arms that has characterized architectural dialogue in the past decades: How can architecture and architects become more relevant to society at large? How can architecture education more realistically prepare young professionals for significant, effective practice?

The responses to these questions have been varied. The UW BASIC Initiative provides an alternative to the traditional education process criticized in publications such as Boyer's report by presenting architectural design as a process that must be learned in part by direct fieldwork; students do real design projects in real communities. The benefits of these collaborative, synthetic learning experiences result not from an artificial educational construct but from the reality of building and working in a poor community. Students not only participate in designing and building a piece of architecture, but upon completion are compelled to reflect on the experience and the outcome of the process and evaluate their design in the context of the "real world."

In locations where physical resources are scarce, human or social capital often replaces economic capital as the primary means for enacting physical change. Students can access this alternative resource while revealing its potential to the community. Recognizing that this is the reality of building in much of the world, the UW BASIC Initiative operates upon the thesis that the informal, nonprofessional sector in these marginalized communities, which accounts for 90 percent of construction in many countries, can be the foundation of a significant educational experience. Additionally, the need to recognize and legitimate the informal sector is a fundamental critique of the current state of high architecture in developing countries and its emphasis on the design studio. Validation for many architecture academies in the developing world comes from following the educational models established by the developed world's institutions, models that focus on styles, and tectonic and material systems which even in the developed world find a limited audience. Placing our classroom in a Mexican squatter settlement, an American Indian reservation, or a U.S. inner city is a response to the rarefied way in which architecture is explored in developed nations.

In our experience, informal and marginalized communities have a healthier connection to architectural initiatives. In the developed world, economic prosperity can encourage a disconnect between high architecture and basic issues of civic importance. Our community studios collectively seek to help reestablish the relevance of poverty to architectural discourse. The UW BASIC Initiative develops direct responses to the realities affecting much of the world's population. The design/build pedagogical structure fosters both technical and social skills, communication and compassion, which equip students for professional practices that are truly connected with and relevant to the world around them. All of the projects profiled in this book have resulted in permanent, vibrant contributions to their host communities.

Young boys on the Pine Ridge Indian Reservation in South Dakota inspect drawings for a new straw-bale house. Photo © 2000 Kate Moxham.

The conception and execution of a building project necessitates a certain level of resolution and real-world understanding of issues not often present in a traditional studio environment, including extreme budget and time constraints, material limitations, and the need to quickly establish a constructive, working dialogue with the client. For many students, this studio presents the first opportunity to undertake a formal design exercise that is informed by these challenges.

The buildings taken on by the BASIC Initiative typically contribute to the long-term viability of the marginalized community by helping them provide for their educational, health, and housing needs. As artifacts, these buildings symbolize the collaborative effort and are an ongoing reminder of the communities' potential for self-sufficiency.

Encouraging Global Citizenship

Invested in the long-term sustainability and survival of all global communities and cultures, the BASIC Initiative engages one of the fundamental questions faced every day by disadvantaged communities worldwide: what makes a sustainable community? Today, many historically sustainable societies in places such as the United States, Mexico, India, and Cuba are in danger of perishing as a consequence of the dramatic upheavals wrought by the world's changing economic, technological, and political environments. As

Volunteers lend a hand during the pour of the slab at Escuela San Lucas. Photo by Byron Baker.

the world's economies become increasingly integrated into a concentrated global market, older societies find themselves unable to compete with the vast resources driving economic globalization and centralization. As a consequence, many communities face the choice of extreme poverty or migration to join the underpaid workforce in urban economic development zones. Once there, stresses increase and isolation, discrimination, and marginalization usually meet the new migrant. As choices become fewer and harder, it is not just the life, but the very livelihood and cultural identity of the community that are put at risk.

The BASIC Initiative believes that in spite of these communities' dire

economic predicament, their traditional knowledge and community-based practices offer the possibility of negotiating a better life. Scratching beneath the surface of poverty, non-governmental organizations working in the world's marginalized communities have, over the last twenty years, consistently found that the real wealth of these communities lies not in their potential as a cheap labor force but in the enduring social practices that enable them to leverage and multiply their meager resources.[3] This unseen fabric of culture (their social capital) is the untapped resource critical to their, and our, world's survival.

The process of undertaking a design/build project in direct engage-

"A school will be built here."

Client: community of San Lucas; Acción y Dessarollo Ecológico

Funding: UW BASIC; Kellogg Foundation; Municipality of Juitepec, Morelos; Cementos de Morelos

Budget: $171,000 ($86,000 for construction of 6 classrooms, bathrooms, and faculty offices; $35,000 for construction of road, basketball courts, and gardens; $29,000 for construction of cistern and biodigester; $18,000 for community sewage and wastewater drainage system; $3,600 for mosaics and metalwork)

Program: 1995: site and community infrastructure, garden pavilion; 1996–97: two elementary school buildings for 320 students

Project Size: buildings: 4,600 sq. ft.; site work: 53,200 sq. ft.

Challenges: difficult physical site; no road access; novice program; emergent relationship with municipality

Lessons: secure community participation as teachers, students, and promoters of long-term sustainable practices; create educational opportunities that immerse architecture students in the sociocultural fabric of the community

Our first Design/Build Mexico project, Escuela San Lucas, is located in Colonia San Lucas, one of many informal settlements of 800,000 people that now merge in Tejalpa, with Cuernavaca to the north. As a result of intense migration from depressed rural areas, Tejalpa's population doubles about every nine or ten years, making it one of the fastest-growing urban areas in North America, and one of the most disadvantaged.

In 1995, the colonia was expanding into the adjacent volcanic fields, whose rocky soils made it one of the most physically difficult sites possible. This neglected corner of Tejalpa was in need of all basic services. To its emerging community, the most urgent need was to build an elementary school. Mexico's federal government had recently denied them one, and residents were worried that their children were going to grow up without a formal education. Gabriela Videla put together a building committee and obtained some donations from the government while we at Design/Build Mexico put together some donations from the United States; this school became the first UW Design/Build Mexico project. Construction of its two classroom wings, community cistern, kiosk, and eco-reserve took three successive winter quarters, from 1995 to 1997.

Design/Build Mexico didn't have a studio space or dormitories at that time, so the students came up with some basic design ideas in a makeshift space and held a community presentation a week after arriving, pasting designs on the wall of a tortilla mill at the only road intersection in the colonia. There we waited with Don Pedro, the community-designated leader of this project, hoping his call for community input would be respected. Slowly, people wandered out of the tortured but beautiful landscape to see what the students had done. Although the Mexicans were kind and full of compliments, few had any idea of what was really going to happen. In those first several days we had sensed little outward interest or support for this project, but soon after our presentation, we arrived on the site to begin work and saw that a small sign was nailed to a tree: *Aquí se construirá una escuela* ("A school will be built here").

Escuela San Lucas began as an infrastructure project. The indigenous communal council of Tejalpa, *los comunideros,* had given land at the edge of the colonia's surrounding volcanic wilderness for the site of the school. As we arrived to start construction in that first year, we were forced to bring materials across the neighboring volcanic field by hand because there was no road connecting it to the site. The first act of solidarity from the community came one Sunday about a week into the project, when community members showed up with sledgehammers and their incredible expertise in cracking giant volcanic boulders. Together we began building what became the main road of the community. Building this road was an essential precursor to the success of the rest of the Escuela San Lucas project. It established that we understood what was significant to these people; students put architecture aside to help build the urban fabric of a community. This atmosphere of trust and mutual understanding started what is still the strongest relationship we've ever had with a community.

After completing the road, the next piece of community infrastructure we tackled was a giant cistern for water collection. The cistern received attention from the community; Mexicans understand cisterns because their communities are built around water. However, another group of students moved away from infrastructure work and started building a pavilion for community events. Perhaps in reaction to the practicality of the road and the cistern, the pavilion is very expressive, with four spiral brick columns that support a thin-shell barrel-vaulted roof. Linda Beaumont, a Seattle artist and Professor Badanes's *compañera*, taught students how to create mosaics using ceramic donated by community residents. The pavilion was decorated with dishes, glasses, bottles, and bathroom tiles (poor people's trash) and the result is a jewel in the landscape. It wasn't what local people expected from public architecture, and it began to draw as much attention and admiration as the cistern. Today, it is a favorite place in the colonia to get married.

Both the practical and the visionary aspects of these initial projects attracted tremendous support from this community. The support came in many forms. Meals began to arrive on Sundays, helping to feed volunteers on the community's collective workday. Soon they appeared also during the week. The men of the community began to organize their work schedules to be able to make a consistent contribution to the construction of the project throughout the week. As a result, by the end of the first year in Tejalpa, a threshold had been reached. Design/Build Mexico was woven into the social fabric of the community and people were coming out to offer their help by the hundreds.

Schools embody a potent meaning in an emerging community. A school represents the opportunity for people to go beyond the limitations of their present conditions. Moving to the city is very traumatic for Mexicans who have left agrarian lives; they leave behind their culture, traditions, and family. The construction of the school meant they were going to get something in return for this sacrifice: their children would have the chance at a better education. In addition, in Mexico the building of a school can often provide informal settlements with access to the political process. Any commitment by

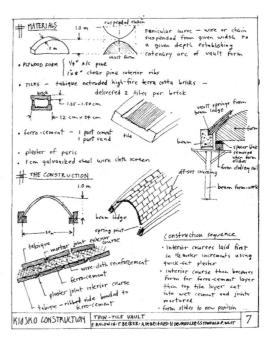

A student drawing explores options for building the vaulted roof of the pavilion. Drawing by Jeffrey Woodward.

I have had many happy memories as a teacher, but the building of this school is unique. There is so much potential in Mexico, but possibilities for a better life often feel like impossibilities. So many things could be achieved if people were focused or had the right attitude, or effort, or even a little money. If you hadn't come with your energy and optimism things wouldn't have changed. The children will be the most affected by this experience; from these classes will come doctors, teachers, and maybe even architects.

We were each trying to solve our problems by ourselves, and you taught us the lesson of collective work: that together we can make a difference in our lives.

Natalia Acuna,
Maestra, Escuela San Lucas

Escuela San Lucas pavilion. Photo by Steve Badanes.

A student decorates the pavilion with broken tiles donated by community members. Photo by Byron Baker.

Photo by Byron Baker.

Photo by Byron Baker.

the government toward education at the new site helps legitimize the settlement as a political entity with the right to ask for representation and further funding. The government's reluctance to fund a school building in San Lucas reflected its desire to limit financial and political liabilities. Once the community found its own means to build a school, the government grudgingly accepted the community as legitimate.

With the beginning of the construction of the school buildings came a legendary teacher, Natalia Acuña, who was already in her fifties and experienced at motivating people. Natalia began to organize the school's future students to participate in construction, forming lines of children carrying buckets full of cement and dirt fill. In addition, we had the luck of hiring a *maestro* (master builder) who came from a big, well-known family. He became a cultural bridge to the members of the community not yet involved, the master masons, as well as a resource for our own students. Thanks to these meaningful partnerships, the construction of this school became the heart of the community's activities during these three years.

As the students learned more about the spirit and experiences of the community, they began to formulate strong ideas about the unusual site. Marked in the center by a large rocky depression, the site presented a serious construction challenge. The community members explained, however, that traditional Aztec schools taught children about their natural environment before they taught them about the higher arts, and the idea emerged to preserve the site topography as we found it. The natural landscape was extraordinary and the people beginning to populate this site had a fundamental understanding of its potential; it made sense to encourage them to maintain the site in its original form rather than level it, and to pass on this legacy of their knowledge of the natural world to their children.

The site was also in the middle of several paths that people had been using for years to harvest roots, vegetables, and herbs. Rather than building walls around it, in keeping with the local tradition, the students chose to leave the site unbounded, with the hope that people could still maintain these paths and ecological practices. The complex landscape was approached as a means by which the school could integrate itself into the cultural memory of the community.

The classroom wings were built in two stages over the next two years of the project. The first school building was constructed of materials produced in the community: concrete blocks; pre-stressed, pre-cast concrete beams; and infill blocks from car decking in nearby parking structures. The building has a linear east-west orientation and a shed roof that protects the classrooms from

Boys explore the volcanic rocks that serve as the foundation for the Escuela San Lucas.

Casa de Salud Malitzin
Ampliación Tejalpa, Tejalpa, Morelos, MEXICO
1998–1999

The perimeter wall and auditorium of the Casa de Salud Malitzin. Photo by Owen Gump.

Client: Promotoras Ambientales de Tejalpa

Funding: Casa de Salud Malitzin· Municipality of Juitepec, Morelos

Budget: $68,600 ($56,000 for buildings; $12,600 for gardens, biodigester, and infrastructure).

Program: health clinic with auditorium, clinical and physical therapy spaces, *temascal* (native steam bath), pharmacy, courtyard, biodigester

Project size: building: 4,200 sq. ft.; site work: 3,600 sq. ft.

Challenges: steep grade on site; polluted site; multiple orientations and street exposures lead to difficult ventilation and solar exposure

Lessons: proactive community interactions (health fairs, open clinic days) engage neighbors in the project; the traditional Mexican courtyard scheme creates a secure and comfortable microclimate

From the start, the family medical clinic in Ampliación Tejalpa presented challenges that distinguished it from the Escuela San Lucas project. San Lucas was an area that was only beginning to develop when Design/Build Mexico arrived, so the program had significant influence on the physical and social fabric of the community. The Casa de Salud Malitzin site in Ampliación Tejalpa, on the other hand, is situated on a corner between three different colonias in Tejalpa, each with its own complicated history of settlement and struggle for political legitimacy. The politics of the area had been controlled by one dominant family for decades. The family's political legitimacy, and by extension that of the entire settlement's, had been challenged by state authorities in the months prior to the clinic project, so the community was feeling embattled and suspicious of outsiders when the design/build studio arrived in 1998.

The need for a clinic, however, was compelling enough to push these impediments aside. Fourteen years earlier, a group of local women led by Estela Bello had organized as Promotoras Ambientales (Women's Environmental Promoters, PAT) of women's health and welfare in the squatter community. They had seen the deepening health crisis that women were facing in Mexico's squatter communities. Due to entrenched ideas of matriarchal self-sacrifice and the lack of resources suffered when moving to the colonias, women were too often the last in the family to receive medical attention. By putting the rest of the family's health first, they were neglecting themselves and putting their children at risk. The *promotoras* started to offer traditional medical services for these women in the front room of one of the member's houses. They were empowering women simply by making them aware of what health options they had, particularly reproductive options, and promoting women's rights in general. Over time, the promotoras expanded the scope of their care-giving by collecting funds and sending representatives to seminars in naturopathic medicine, expanding their knowledge and formalizing their qualifications. This continued presence and growing agenda made the clinic an increasingly important community resource over the years. After witnessing the Escuela San Lucas project, the promotoras approached the Design/Build Mexico program and suggested we make a women's health clinic our next studio project.

Even though we had established ourselves in the community through the Escuela San Lucas project, which was only about a kilometer away, there was considerable suspicion about us at this new site, due to the ongoing political issues with the state. In the first month we worked mostly by ourselves, with only a few community members offering help. However, we had an enthusias-

A weekend health fair brings nursing students and community residents to the Casa de Salud for pet vaccinations and general health information.

The various buildings that make up the clinic gather around a peaceful central courtyard. Photo by Owen Gump.

The school building that preceded Escuela Castellanos on this site was constructed of slats from fruit packing crates.

Client: Comunidad; Colonia Cuauhtémoc Cárdenas

Funding: UW BASIC; Alfred Zuckolov Foundation; Ministry of Education, Morelos; Municipality of Juitepec, Morelos

Budget: $138,000 ($96,000 for buildings; $20,000 for sewage and infrastructure; $12,000 for walls, gardens, and playground)

Program: elementary school for approximately 360 students

Project size: building: 3,600 sq. ft.; site work: 128,000 sq. ft.

Challenges: must meet standards and codes set by Mexico's Ministry of Education; must keep existing school open during construction

Lessons: communicate more effectively with government agencies (Ministry of Education)

Escuela Rosario Castellanos in Colonia Cuauhtémoc Cárdenas is at the edge of Cuernavaca's informal settlements on land adjacent to CIVAC, the city's industrial sector. CIVAC is dominated by export-driven manufacturers of pharmaceuticals, textiles, and numerous other consumer goods. Like the communities we had worked in earlier, this informal settlement was built on unclaimed land at the edge of this industrial sector, purely because of local people's initiative. What is unique about Capiri is that it is both more established and more sparse than adjacent colonias. Unlike San Lucas, which was an empty field when we arrived, the site of Cuauhtémoc Cárdenas had been settled for fifteen years; however, it had never achieved full density, because of an ongoing conflict in character and ideology between it and the adjacent planned housing community. Cuauhtémoc Cárdenas was a fragment firmly positioned at the extreme edge of several already tenuous urban settlements. As the frontier to the "official" housing built by the industries of CIVAC, people were wary of being too close to the factories and their dominant influence.

This project began thanks to a generous donation by Alfred Zuckolov, an optician and inventor from New Hampshire. Through his marriage to a Mexican woman, he came to meet the people of Comunidad, the Cuernavaca organization assembled by Gabriela Videla after the success of Escuela San Lucas to promote development in squatter settlements. In one of those encounters, he visited the squatter communities where we had been working and met a disabled child who, because of his disabilities, could not attend school. Zuckolov had been so taken by the plight of the child that he wanted to fund a school that would be accessible to this and all future children with disabilities. He was also unwilling to wait more than a year for the building, so he put a condition on his gift: we needed to complete a working school within nine weeks of our program. This condition made the project one of the most ambitious we have undertaken in a single program period.

There was a makeshift but well-attended school on the Escuela Castellanos site when Design/Build Mexico arrived, built by the community years earlier with extremely limited means. The walls were made of wooden fruit boxes, the slats of which had been taken apart and reassembled to form a long, narrow schoolroom. The thin wooden slats admitted an incredibly soft and beautiful but distracting light. It was a dangerously fragile structure with no windows and patched-in electricity. But 180 students and five teachers were making it work as a school. Our project would double the number of students receiving an education at the site. Throughout the construction of the new school building, classes continued in this space.

The north building of Escuela Castellanos was built entirely by UW BASIC students and community members.

The south building was built by the Ministry of Education, who made the mistake of reversing the UW BASIC students' design, so that it maximizes solar exposure. Photo by Owen Gump.

That year we had a very unified design process. Using large drawings and models developed in conjunction with the children and parents of the school, we involved the community more closely in the design process than in previous programs. As the design moved toward the final proposal, we brought in the community and the teachers to offer their opinions at different stages. Many important issues about the size of classrooms and outdoor spaces emerged in the discussions. Because of the ongoing conflict with neighboring "official" housing settlements, the community also insisted that the school be walled in and protected from vandalism. This last requirement changed the nature of the school significantly, as the students had initially been inspired by the open campus of the Escuela San Lucas. To resolve this, students chose to make the entrance an event: as you penetrate the exterior wall, you find yourself on a bridge over a series of gardens that run the entire perimeter of the school walls. This planting diffuses the view of the wall from the gardens and allows each classroom to have its own small teaching garden in back. In combination with the bougainvilleas on the trellis in front, they wrap the classrooms in a cooling green shade and create the sense of learning in nature.

The building itself was also inspired by the second phase of the Escuela San Lucas, using similar extended fins to protect the school from the heat of the western setting sun. The building is positioned along the east-west axis, with a sloping shed roof that creates a low overhang to the south, shielding the classrooms from direct sunlight, and that opens up in the rear of the building to permit northern light. Punched openings in the fins on the south side create the shared commons of a wide corridor that runs along the length of the building. The shed roof allows for ventilation, capturing dominant winds from the south and pushing hot air out ventilated casement windows at the north. When the winds reverse, the air is cooled on its way in by shady gardens at the rear of the building and let out near the courtyard. The building works superbly in terms of passive cooling and lighting.

The very formal principal, Irma Mendoza, was both supportive of the process and suspicious of what we would do, despite her awareness of our success at San Lucas. As opposed to Natalia Acuña, the maestra from San Lucas who had been raised in the revolutionary rural school tradition and spent a lifetime devoted to community efforts, Irma believed in the established school model of the Ministry of Education. For instance, the shed-roof form of the building design, which worked so well environmentally, created a huge conflict with the Ministry of Education and with Irma's idea of what a school should look like. They wanted our students to change the roof to a traditional gable form to look more like the school prototypes the

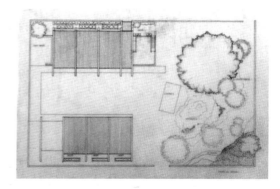

Site plan, Escuela Castellanos.

A colorín tree, whose flowers are harvested by locals for making dyes and traditional winter food, sits on the site intended for this primary school. The tree is an important symbol and resource for the poor community, but the school is desperately needed. Moving the site of the school to save the tree would push the volunteer project beyond its budget. The discussion amongst students this afternoon is heated as they try to decide what to do. With night pending, the group finally resolves itself on the side of economics. It has not been an easy decision, and many in the group feel that the program's principles and the message to the community have been compromised.

Dave, Jeff, and Mark have walked two miles to find a taxi rather than have to endure the forty-five minute bus ride on bad roads back to the dormitories.

"So you are the Americanos building the school," says the taxi driver, looking back. The three, a little astounded, nod.

"I heard you guys decided to cut down the colorín. I wouldn't have even given it a thought," he says. "What's so important about that tree?"

The three look at each other, exhausted.

To enter the school, one passes through the thickness of the north building into the courtyard. Photo by Owen Gump.

Students spend a day at work with family farmers in the cooperative. Photo by Holly Batt.

Seattle artist Linda Beaumont creates a mosaic that is part of the renovation of the chicken coop.

Students build the double roof that will transform the interior space of the coop, creating a heat break that keeps the space cool.

we found alternate solutions. We ended up doing everything through acts of solidarity, gathering materials from anywhere we could. It became a true scrounge act, which was a valuable lesson for students who had normally worked in places where a variety of construction materials were available. They became committed to limiting material demands through careful design and then fulfilling them with recycled or nontraditional materials.

Our building site was in a community of agricultural workers tending what are considered to be large urban plots, two- to three-acre farms carved out of the former wealthy estate neighborhoods of Havana. We were given an old industrial chicken coop that we renovated into a semi-open-air meeting hall, our first big recycling move. The large, rectangular building was essentially a huge roof on four posts with limited wall exposure. As in our Mexico projects, heat gain was a major concern. The existing corrugated roof offered great shade, but at the same time conducted most of the sun's heat into the space. The students designed a solution in which they hung Masonite ceiling panels from the existing roof structure, creating a double layer between the interior and the hot sun. The air between the layers created a heat break, which was ventilated through the roof. Helping to deflect the heat between the layers was a reflective barrier that one of our Cuban collaborators had crossed half the island to find and acquire in exchange for 80 chickens. Since the usual cylindrical sonotubes were not available, the smaller entrance pergolas and inner roofs were constructed on concrete columns that were poured into large, locally harvested timber bamboo as formwork. The result was a shady, comfortable pavilion for meetings and events.

Students envisioned the project as one that would help promote and celebrate the rich variety of social groups engaged in urban agriculture in Seattle and Havana. To this end, Seattle artist Linda Beaumont joined us once again and brought 300 pounds of recycled hand-blown Seattle glass. With the students, she created rich mosaics on the front facade of the building, which overlooks a large terrace of recycled brick. The terrace acts as an outdoor meeting space under the shade of an allée of trees. Surrounding the entire construction is a garden, designed by the landscape architecture students, that wraps the building in the colors of the Cuban flag when it flowers.

Overall, the building diagram is very simple, as one would expect from a three-week project. While the mosaic and garden function to celebrate the space, the real lessons came from simply trying to create architecture based primarily on the human and intellectual capacity of the students and our collaborators in the agricultural community. We had never had to do so much with so little, and this was an experience that dramatically affected our students and program. The subsequent library they designed and built in the remaining seven weeks in Mexico showed a greater degree of economy of labor and material than we ever had seen before, and yet the architecture was just as compelling as any of our other buildings. We had to believe these were the lessons of Cuba.

During our final celebration at the Chief Seattle Social Club, as the Urban Organic Agricultural Center came to be christened, the cooperative's thirty-six local farmers joined hundreds of others who will be served by the center. The farmers cooked swordfish and pig over an open fire using the metal frame and springs from an old mattress as a barbecue grate. This makeshift but effective oven was the perfect example of what it means to live and work in Cuba, and the memorable taste of that food was testimony that sometimes less is more.

A student wheels in cement as Che Guevara looks on. Photo by Holly Batt.

Students build a bio-swale to provide the gardens with water.

Biblioteca Pública Municipal Juana de Asbaje y Ramírez
Colonia Joya de Agua, Juitepec, Morelos, MEXICO
2001

Photo by Owen Gump.

Photo by Owen Gump.

Client: Municipality of Juitepec, Morelos

Funding: Municipality of Juitepec, Morelos; Federal Assistance to Cities, Mexico; UW BASIC

Budget: $56,000 ($40,000 for building; $12,000 for shelving and library equipment; $4,000 for gardens and perimeter wall)

Community Partner: Comunidad

Program: children's library

Project size: building: 1,617 sq. ft.; site work: 1,260 sq. ft.

Challenges: short six-week work period; making curved forms with unit masonry; incorporating the skills of our artists in residence

Lesson: simple, expressive building diagrams allow swift but meaningful results

The Biblioteca Pública Municipal Juana de Asbaje y Ramírez in Colonia Joya de Agua sits in a small, rural community with 800 to 1,000 inhabitants at the very edge of the town of Juitepec. Almost lost in a large, pastoral valley, Juitepec was once known for great estates created around the ruins of old sugar mills as fantasy palaces for the internationally wealthy. Today it is still one of the city's most prosperous suburbs, but also one of the fastest-growing urban areas in North America. Perched alongside this realm of plenty is the little village of Joya de Agua, which houses working people employed in the industrial sector of CIVAC. Although the colonia is modest, CIVAC supplements its economic shortfalls, and therefore it has fairly good services and is relatively uncontaminated, in contrast to previous GCS sites.

This library project came out of a long-term struggle of a group of mothers in the community that had championed books and reading from the first year of the Escuela San Lucas project. Comunidad had taken on their cause and had attempted through various means to get the municipality of Juitepec to fund both children's and municipal libraries for the colonias. By 2000, a new, more receptive administration had taken over and offered some support if the design/build program would agree to do the work, a move they knew would gain them political legitimacy, another sign of the growing importance of our work in these colonias.

There were very few libraries in any of Cuernavaca's squatter communities. The city was in the midst of building a large general library downtown, but people in the squatter settlements, particularly children, have limited or no access to central Cuernavaca. Buses cost several precious pesos, and most children, whose parents work all day, often cannot ride alone. In addition, schools in these communities rarely have library collections. This leaves 300,000 to 400,000 children in the squatter communities without easy access to books.

During a slide presentation about our program in my twins' fourth-grade class in Seattle, I happened to mention this library idea. The fourth-graders were immediately touched by the notion that there were children elsewhere without libraries in their schools. One little girl raised her hand and said she had a lot of extra books she didn't need and she would like to donate them, and before I knew it, the entire class was making pledges and offering to come down to build the library themselves. When our university students and the people at Comunidad in Cuernavaca heard about this enthusiasm, they were convinced this would make a great design/build project. The elementary school in Seattle took on a book donation campaign, and we made the library the 2001 Design/Build Mexico project.

What distinguishes Joya de Agua is both its geographic isolation among

The civic building serves as an entry marker to the playfields beyond. Photo by Owen Gump.

The building's form mimics the surrounding foothills. Photo by Owen Gump.

Landscape architecture students incorporated broken glass tiles into the design of the entry courtyard.

The U.S. Pavilion sits amid a dry plain in an undeveloped quadrant of Auroville. Photo by Pino Marchese.

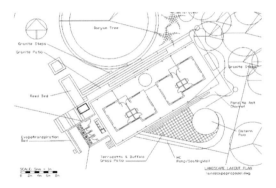

Site plan, U.S. Pavilion.

Client: Auroville International, USA; City of Auroville

Funding: UW BASIC; Auroville International, USA; UW Provost Office; private donations

Budget: $216,000 ($80,000 for building; $28,000 for roof system; $16,000 for sitework and dams; $9,200 for solar energy system; $8,600 for composting toilets and waste treatment program; $6,000 for well)*

Program: dormitory building for 16 students; waste, water, and power infrastructure

Project Size: building: 2,760 sq. ft.; site work and infrastructure: 4,300 sq. ft.

Challenges: difficult permitting process; time lost to effects of travel, design charrette held site-unseen

Lessons: "developing world" is a superb classroom for exploring sustainable practices, thanks to simple, underdeveloped infrastructures

*Figures do not reflect 100 percent of budget total

After years of working in marginalized, informal communities in Mexico, an international community in the southern Indian state of Tamil Nadu presented a dramatic change of venue for the GCS program. Started in 1962 by Europeans studying the teachings of the Sri Aurobindo ashram in Pondicherry, the city of Auroville was founded on the principles of Sri Aurobindo's most influential student, known as "the Mother." She envisioned Auroville as an international center of human unity that would one day have 50,000 inhabitants. Today it has 2,000 permanent residents from six continents, 50 percent of whom are Indian, and covers about 30 square miles of land. Its citizens support themselves through agriculture, industries such as textile production for export, and professional sciences in sustainability design and computer technologies. In this sense, it resembles many other boom towns in Southern India, such as Pondicherry or Hyderabad.

Auroville is well-funded by both private and public institutions, and residents combine these resources to do *karma yoga,* or "life work," directed towards furthering the city's development. Citizenship in the community must be sponsored by another member of the community and only happens after a period when one's contributions or karma yoga is judged to be a worthy contribution. They interpret the goal of human unity in a number of ways, including cultural and environmental sustainability and social equality and awareness. The community's most famous work is the ongoing forty-year reforestation effort it undertook upon incorporation, which began in the immediate vicinity and later spread all over the state of Tamil Nadu. Auroville is credited with completely revitalizing the landscape of this state through the planting of millions of trees.

Auroville is still largely rural, and, rather than developing within a framework of infrastructure, seems to grow in small unrelated parcels when specific funding is granted. The Mother's vision included a section of the city that would become the international district, providing housing and meeting space for visitors from around the world. In 2001 several donors gave money for the construction of a U.S. pavilion. A previous delegation of students, from the University of Washington Comparative History of Ideas program, heard about the project and put Auroville representatives in touch with Design/Build Mexico.

The decision to accept this project for the 2002 design/build studio was not easy. For years, we had been working in very poor communities, where our contributions fulfilled serious needs. Auroville is a well-funded community surrounded by people in serious need, and the well-funded portion would be the client for this project. On the other hand, the site, like most of

Auroville, was completely without infrastructure, and this building would challenge our students to provide energy, water, and waste solutions that would test the design/build program's commitment to environmental sustainability. We asked the Auroville representatives to find funding for a similar project that would benefit the local villages, thereby establishing a better link between this international community and the Indian community, and better fulfilling our commitment to cultural sustainability. But the available funds had been specifically donated, by U.S. supporters of Auroville, to create a study center and facility for Americans (both North and South) to live in while studying in Auroville and Southern India, and we were not allowed much flexibility to reinterpret their intended use. In the end, the opportunity to contribute an alternative model of infrastructure development that would serve to address Auroville, rural India, and many of the communities we serve worldwide by developing a building which was totally off the grid was too much of an educational opportunity for us to pass by. There was also the opportunity to learn from Auroville's and Southern India's strong legacy in use of traditional sustainable materials. All this became evident to us, despite the shortcomings, when in January of 2001 Professor Charles Henry first came to explore the educational potential of this commission.

While India is much less technologically developed than Mexico or Cuba, it has a lot of people (fifteen times the population density of Mexico) and therefore ample labor and ample red tape. It was the red tape that first made an impression. In Mexico, students had been able to design a building during a two-week-long charrette held when we first arrived. As soon as they finished designing, we would break ground. Working in informal settlements, we avoided any formal design review or official supervision; like most squatters, we simply built on the land the community had designated; Mexico's unique land ownership laws allowed for this. In Auroville, we had to submit plans for approval well in advance of construction, and this meant scheduling our design charrette for the summer preceding the program. The thirty-seven students met without ever having seen the site to design a building for a culture they couldn't possibly understand. The intellectual and practical challenges were immense.

In September of 2001, a second delegation of three faculty members— Jim Adamson, Steve Badanes, and Jason Manges—traveled to India to present the students' design to the Auroville review panel and to research practical construction matters. They were met with mixed news: the resources available for construction looked good, but the building plans didn't. The panel of Aurovilleans overseeing the project felt that the building didn't express

Students work to complete a rammed earth wall.

I've never traveled to India before. I've never been out of America before. This is my first big trip around the world. It's a big project and there's a lot of work, and it's taking place outside of a lot of my comfort zones. This is the first real-world project where I've been able to apply the things that I know. I've been pulling from a lot of what I've learned in school—not just from books, but all the things I've learned socially.

Troy Coleman
Student, Design/Build India

Mimicking a southern Indian banyan tree, the super-roof creates shady verandas on either side of the dorm rooms. Photo by Pino Marchese.

Steel, ferro-cement, rammed earth, and mahogany come together to create a rich palette of local materials. Photos by Pino Marchese.

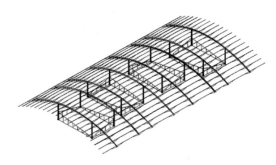

Students engineered the super-roof with the help of local engineers.

Photo © 2003 Nilauro Markus.

identity of Auroville. After some quick design development by the faculty delegation, the panel provisionally approved the building. This bought us the time we needed to redesign on-site, in the manner of our Mexico studio, when we arrived in India with the students.

Geographically and culturally, India is much farther from the United States than Mexico, so our normal breakneck pace had to be slowed upon arrival in Auroville. The first order of business was allowing students time to get their feet on the ground. Once everyone was settled with living quarters in the different communities of Auroville, and given bicycles for transportation, we visited the site and started rethinking this building. By week two we were building.

The site struck us initially as large, flat, and dry. It was about a quarter-mile off the nearest dirt road, but could be reached by an informal yak trail. There was only one building visible from the site, the Tibetan Pavilion, another member of the future Auroville international district. This was by far the flattest, most empty site we'd ever been given. The first challenge for the students was to design a building that would anchor itself in the landscape and culture of Auroville so we wouldn't end up with a figural mass floating in an empty field. The students used the metaphor of an Indian banyan tree as the dominant building concept. Trees in general have immense symbolic importance in Auroville, thanks to the years of reforestation work, and because the city is planned around a giant banyan tree, this species was considered spiritually important by the Mother. Our site had several small trees on its periphery, but was still largely used for cattle grazing and therefore was primarily unvegetated.

The design called for a series of four small dorm rooms set beneath a giant, separate super-roof, to create the same quality of an "outdoor room" that a banyan tree provides in this climate. The design has the usual east-west linear orientation, presenting its broad front to the soft sunlight from the north. The super-roof shades most of the hot Indian sun, allowing penetration only at dusk and dawn. The dorm rooms are built of heavy, earthy materials: mud bricks and rammed earth. The super-roof is built of light-weight steel and wood. In this way, the dorms seem to rise from the ground like a trunk, while the massive roof seems to hover lightly above, like branches and foliage. Each dorm room has a roof of its own, constructed of ferro-cement in the shape of a hyperbolic parabola. These four smaller roof forms seem to rest gently on the chunky building walls, suggesting leaves falling from a tree.

Every decision made in the siting and design of the building was meant to

The dorm rooms find protection under the canopy of the super-roof. Photo by Pino Marchese.

The cantenary sheets of ferrocement gently rest on the rammed earth walls. Photo © 2003 Nilauro Markus.

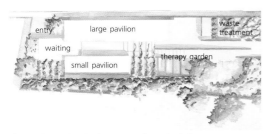

Site plan, Unidad Básica de Rehabilitación.

The quarry face of red quartz marble, found by students on-site, greets patients as they enter the courtyard. Photo by Owen Gump.

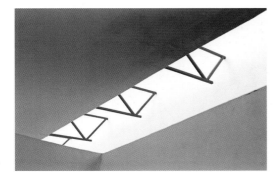

Sunlight floods the light monitor. Photo by Owen Gump.

The resulting building is a pair of long, narrow pavilions that run parallel to the street, with a long courtyard between, around which circulation takes place. The pavilions each house examination and therapy spaces. A third, open pavilion completes the circulation on the north end of the courtyard and houses the waiting room. The entry slips between the natural red-rock wall of the waiting room and the pavilion that borders the street. The entire U-shaped complex and the courtyard it surrounds are at the same grade as the street, so that a person dropped off at the entry can enter without having to use ramps. This works well both for people in wheelchairs and people on crutches, for whom ramps are particularly challenging. The complex is open to the south, allowing the courtyard to extend to a series of gardens accessible by long ramps, a court for wheelchair basketball, and a large planted mulch bed that is an integral part of the building's waste treatment system. This portion of the site is joined to the building by a high perimeter wall, so that the entire complex is private. The ramping system that makes the gardens accessible is envisioned as part of the process of activity and treatment essential to physical therapy, while the courtyard within the U-shaped complex shares the grade of the buildings and is therefore always easily accessible.

The walls of the building are constructed of local stone and masonry block covered with stucco, except for one red-rock wall carefully detailed with recessed mortar joints on the street side of the waiting room. This wall, made of a beautiful vein of red quartz marble found by students at the nearby quarry, welcomes visitors as they approach the entry of the building. The wall vanishes into the first pavilion, suggesting the layering of building forms that make up the larger complex, and allowing the building to seamlessly merge with its gardens. The large stucco wall of the first pavilion that runs along the street is largely solid, in Mexican fashion, except for two long glass-block openings that bring light along the floor of the therapy spaces. Directly on the inside of this high wall, however, is a large monitor that caps the entire length of the pavilion and brings a carefully determined amount of light and air into the building throughout the day. The roofs of the two pavilions are formed by a series of orange steel trusses that are exposed at the building fascia and the vent. In all of our projects, we emphasize the need to calculate and design for the maximum natural lighting conditions. It is an easy, low-cost means of enhancing the quality of our buildings by keeping their energy needs to a minimum. We studied the natural lighting of this building more extensively than on previous projects. Using lighting models and solar calculations of the sun's path during different periods of the year, the students arrived at the monitor's design and window placement, though these designs

Photo by Owen Gump.

Two large folding doors open to provide access between the indoor and outdoor physical therapy spaces. Photo by Owen Gump.

remained contested to the very end. Today the extraordinary natural lighting of the interiors is a tribute to the depth of these design explorations.

Although the students designed every inch of the site and building complex, they built only the larger pavilion along the street. For this reason, the students programmed the spaces so that the first pavilion houses everything needed to run the abbreviated clinic: an interim waiting room, an administration office, two examination rooms, and a large physical therapy room. When the subsequent portions of the building are complete in 2004, the waiting room and administration will move, and the first pavilion will be entirely devoted to examination and therapy spaces.

Among Piñero's other hopes for Xochitepec is the desire to see the town move away from the pollution-prone wastewater treatment systems it currently uses. Most houses use either faulty septic tanks that release unclean water into the groundwater table, or link into ineffective public waste treatment systems that divert mostly unclean water into rivers and streams. The mayor wanted us to build a system for this building that would be a low-cost example for the community, much like the one we built in Auroville the previous year. Mark Merkelbach, a graduate student from the Auroville program, returned as a teaching assistant for this year's Mexico program and, along with Professor Henry, led a student group in the design and construction of a waste treatment system. The system uses large settling tanks and a giant planted mulch bed to complete the treatment of partially clean wastewater coming from the building's standard septic tank.

The construction of this building reflected a constant struggle between a stubborn site and a well-intentioned design. The two primary requirements of the program, accessibility and innovative wastewater treatment, meant that even with a careful, well-considered design and grading plan, we had to move huge amounts of earth without disturbing the large trees on-site in order to accomplish our goals. The energy expended during the initial weeks of the project matched any of our earlier work. Students took away the understanding that when a given site isn't ideal, one must calculate the return on energy invested in changing it. In this case, we believe the investment was worthwhile, as evidenced by pictures of the building in use and making a positive impact on the community just three weeks after our departure.

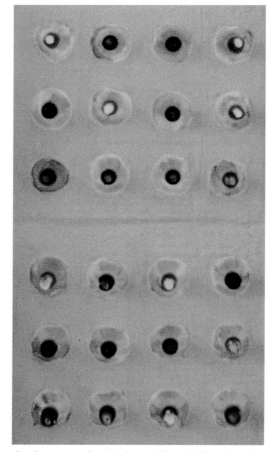

Students created a window of discarded beer bottles. Photo by Owen Gump.

The existing worker cabins made a challenging starting point.

Client: Aristeo Maldonado and family

Funding: UW BASIC; UW Department of Architecture; UW Department of Construction Management

Budget: $5,900 for materials

Program: common spaces for existing migrant housing; experimental straw-bale housing unit

Challenges: small budget made material resourcefulness essential; academic schedule limited the amount of time students could spend on-site

Lessons: a good working relationship with the client helps overcome material limitations; even small interventions inspire the clients to make larger physical improvements down the road

The migrant housing situation was just coming to a state of publicized crisis in the summer of 1997, when we undertook our first migrant community project in Eastern Washington. Tens of thousands of migrants were camping along the fruit-producing river valleys of Washington. These encampments had few real services and were, as a consequence, severely impacting the environmental quality of rivers and small farming communities in the region. Although this situation had been going on for decades, the number of immigrants was growing with the increased fruit production of the region in the last twenty years. A series of Pulitzer Prize–winning newspaper articles by the *Seattle Times* in 1997 and prominent letters to national newspapers were finally introducing the issue to the general public.

Keenly aware of the problem and wanting to help, the UW BASIC Initiative had taken the risk of organizing a design/build studio without our usual level of advance preparation or a solid partnering organization. The migrant worker housing problem proved harder to engage than we had imagined; two weeks into our program, we still had no one willing to work with us—both farmers and activists had become so overwhelmed by the new visibility of the problem that they were reluctant to invite a student project into their midst.

Our first project came to us by chance. A priest who had been instrumental in publicizing the migrant worker housing dilemma introduced us to the Maldonados. The Maldonados were a family of migrant field workers who, after nearly two decades as manual laborers, were able to purchase an apple orchard on the Okanogan River in sparsely populated Okanogan County through a low-interest federal loan program. To keep their debt as low as possible, they had chosen to sell off the main house and were living in one of the farm's six worker cabins; they were twelve people making the most out of less than 500 square feet. Despite their own living conditions, the family felt they wanted to offer an act of solidarity to fellow migrant farmers by offering improved working and living conditions on their own farm. Thus, the first studio began as an investigation of the life of migrant workers and the ways in which architecture could improve conditions.

To acquaint students with a lifestyle they knew little about, we asked them to get to know the Maldonado family and other farm workers by living on the farm over several extended weekends. Framing the studio problem as a study of a way of life led to some unexpected observations and ideas for interventions. The studio developed not only plans for the five units of housing but also smaller interventions that addressed the everyday routines and social patterns of the small community.

The houses were envisioned as small 350-square-foot straw-bale structures

Maldonado Farm as work began.

This old truck became a community barbecue that sits at the end of the shaded porch.

with shed roofs. They were to be organized in clusters around outdoor social spaces. Time and zoning restrictions meant that we were only able to design the housing, but we were able to both design and build the smaller interventions.

The outdoor interventions included shaded porches and trellises for the adjoining cabins, a shaded rest stop with a solar oven for lunchtime breaks, a large porch and barbecue, an indoor basketball court, a cantilevered pier for fishing in the river, and a laundry room. The cantilevered pier and trellises were inspired by Japanese bypass construction, which eliminates the need to cut wood to precise measurements, thereby accommodating students' novice skill level while still achieving beautiful results. Farmers and migrants participated in the pouring of the footings for the pier, which became the social capital-building event we had hoped would draw on the clients' Mexican heritage, and got the Maldonado's children involved showing students how to do it properly. The porch and trellis frame a courtyard that creates a recognizable symbolic center for the community.

Students were inspired by the landscape of semiarid canyon walls, mesas, and fertile valleys below, as well as the functionality and resource efficiency of the farms. As a result, students reused materials from the site, such as the carcass of a 1950s Dodge pickup truck that they painted bright yellow and whose hood opened to reveal the community barbecue. The pickup was parked at the end of the new porch the students had attached to the largest barn—a sculpture for the center of the newly formed *placita* (courtyard) in the middle of the housing units.

By the end of the project, local farmers and representatives from the state government were coming by to witness our progress and to discuss future collaborations. Despite the slow start and reduced scale of this project, it established our program within Eastern Washington farming communities and laid the groundwork for subsequent projects.

In 1999, MWHI returned to the Maldonado farm and, in a series of two weekends, finally built the model migrant housing units the family had always wanted. In a demonstration project during a research seminar on straw-bale construction offered by Professors David Wiley, Penelope West, and myself, we were able to illustrate our housing solutions to a larger farming community. Through experimental straw-bale technology, we were able to prove that housing can be built of waste material in a weekend by volunteer labor, in this case students of the seminar and the Maldonado family.

Aluminum poles and colored canvas form a shaded rest stop for lunch breaks.

An old warehouse was converted into a day-lit indoor basketball court.

Students designed experimental housing units that employ straw-bale technology.

A student's diagram illustrates the construction sequence of the experimental housing units. Drawings by Brendan Connolly.

Photo by Krishna Bharathi.

Peggy White House
Garryowen, Montana
1999

Photo by Owen Gump.

Peggy White's grandparents' home sits down the road. Photo by Owen Gump.

Client: Peggy White and family

Funding: UW Department of Architecture; UW Department of Construction Management; Red Feather Development Group; Kelly Foundation; McMillan Truss; Home Depot of Billings, Montana

Budget: $51,000

Program: straw-bale house for a single mother and her children

Project Size: building: 1,400 sq. ft.; site work: 860 sq. ft.

Challenges: first AIHI straw-bale project; climate and time constraints; heavy trusses inappropriate for volunteer labor force

Lessons: advance preparation essential to student success with a new technology; May in Montana is too rainy and windy for volunteer construction; decent housing can truly change a person's life

This one-and-a-half-story, three-bedroom straw-bale home represented the first of its kind in Montana and offered the first large-scale opportunity for students to test theories about straw-bale construction generated by our earlier demonstration efforts in eastern Washington. Peggy White was the ideal first client for a housing type that was entirely new and somewhat experimental at this stage in this region—she was open to adventure. A warm, vocal, gregarious, and popular woman, Peggy had waited years on the Crow Housing Authority housing rolls. She was thrilled about finally getting her new house.

The site for Peggy's house is only a couple hundred yards from Interstate 90, on land that has been in her family for years. The remnants of her grandparents' log house stands about a quarter-mile down the highway. The land is flat, relatively unforested, and lies very low in the water table. The microclimate was a dramatic location for working and camping; the ground was often damp, and biting winds tore across the plain throughout the build. Offsetting these challenges was the fact that the site borders a huge highway, which made the straw-bale process highly visible to passersby. While not the perfect home site for everyone, it was ideal for Peggy, with her outgoing personality.

This first AIHI project took place during the spring academic quarter. We chose spring because we imagined this studio someday becoming part of the regular academic offerings in construction management and in architecture at both Penn State and Washington. Summer is a time when many of our students work to cover their academic expenses. This first studio took on an ambitious agenda: designing the house and construction details; planning, executing, and managing the construction process; and investigating the few straw-bale codes throughout the states to see what normative values and conventions had been established elsewhere. This last research was particularly important because, through this house and others that followed, we meant to establish a viable housing program for Native Americans of this region, and this meant standardization. The work in these four areas was conducted by groups of students (often from both construction management and architecture) during the five weeks we prepared for the build. Constant planning meetings and informal exchanges created a sense of a team approach before we even arrived at the site in early May.

Prior to the two-week blitz build, an advance local prep team built the foundation and platform so that when the students arrived the walls could go up immediately. This has become standard practice in our two-week summer builds because site preparation and foundation pouring are labor intensive, time consuming, and do not teach students as much as the rest of the process.

May in Montana can be cold, rainy, and windy. Photo by Michael Rosenberg.

Students work well into twilight hours. Photo by Michael Rosenberg.

The straw-bale walls rise. Photo © 2000 Kate Moxham.

achieving a fourteen-day completion time.

At the beginning of the build, students were asked to break into groups and take control of a specific aspect of the construction process, such as wall assembly or stick framing. As that particular stage of construction neared, the group met with the professors to plan the upcoming task. Then, when the time for that task arrived, they trained the rest of the students and the volunteer labor group. The process worked so well, it has been used on most of our subsequent programs.

Thanks to the spring quarter spent planning the project, the build itself went quickly and efficiently; the walls, central utility core, and roof of the single-story, two-bedroom house went up in fourteen days, as planned. In the end, the design improvements decreased costs and increased the use of community and volunteer labor by limiting the technical steps in the construction process. Volunteer labor provided by Red Feather Development Group and St. Thomas Moore Church of Darien, Connecticut, proved not only helpful to our team but rewarding to the volunteers themselves because the construction process was so clear that the work always had an obvious purpose and effect.

In terms of physical conditions, the build couldn't have differed more from that of Peggy White's house the preceding year. Scorching heat replaced rain and wind and made the construction process challenging in different ways. The critical stucco application was hindered because the hot sun dried the stucco before it was spread properly. In response, twenty-seven graduate and undergraduate students worked in the dark of early morning or the evening to stucco the building. Once the process got back on track, the Fast Wolfs' grandchildren joined the students on-site and created murals in the stucco by molding it with their hands, telling the story of the migration of the Dakota Sioux across the plains to this part of South Dakota.

At the conclusion of the project, students met for another short seminar at the university. They proposed further changes and improvements to the design. These included increasing the size of the home to match the average needs of families on reservations, maintaining the concept of the core, and generating additional drawings and specifications to describe the design to the various lay groups that take part in community-built projects. The 2000 build developed what became a yearly cycle in our AIHI program: learning about the technology, building, reflecting on the build, and refining the prototype. Straw-bale technology is underresearched and in many ways it is a system that needs to be built then designed, rather than designed and built. Students inverted our mantra and coined the term "build/design" for the AIHI studios.

Photo © 2000 Kate Moxham.

We funded one of our latest development projects, but were required to get IHS's [Indian Housing Service, a federal agency] blessing on it, if you will. So they came in, engineered it, designed it, and oversaw construction of it. We've had systems fail and when we try to take them to the carpet on it, they say, "It's yours. We didn't have a whole lot to do with it; we just designed it." We didn't include IHS in the last project we did. We hired our own engineering firm and worked with their design, because at least a private company has an obligation.

We're going to give IHS the opportunity to work together again on this next project we're doing. I'm optimistic, but yet there's part of me that says, "Okay, when does this relationship break?" As long as they can keep making it appear that we're not competent, then they've always got a job. I call this the "Mother, may I?" syndrome.

Mike Speelman
Modernization Coordinator, Northern Cheyenne Housing Authority

Students stucco after sunset to avoid the scorching heat, which dries the stucco too quickly. Photo © 2000 Kate Moxham.

Photo © 2000 Kate Moxham.

Site walls create wind breaks which allow a warm microclimate to emerge around the house during winter. Photo © 2000 Kate Moxham.

Windows for this public building were a full bale larger than windows in previous residential projects.

Client: Chief Dull Knife Memorial College

Funding: USDA grant to Tribal Colleges; Penn State University (PSU) Honors College; PSU College of Architectural Engineering; UW College of Architecture and Urban Planning; Oprah Winfrey; Red Feather Development Group

Budget: $225,000

Program: adult education and literacy center

Project size: building: 1,400 sq. ft.; site work: 960 sq. ft.

Challenges: spatially complex public building; extremely large group of students and volunteers

Lessons: keep groups smaller; offer opportunities for cultural immersion away from building site

The Adult Education Center at Chief Dull Knife College departs from the usual AIHI commitment to housing; instead we built a small community building for the college that is used as a resource center for adults interested in improving their reading and writing skills. It is the first AIHI project led by a partnership between the UW BASIC Initiative and Penn State.

The project partners took on this community building in hopes of engaging tribal members in the straw bale building process at a larger scale than had been possible in the previous single-family house builds. Although we still envisioned straw bale technology as having the potential to vastly influence American Indian housing, we felt that a public building would be a great venue for getting the community more involved in the technology. A private home serves one family's needs; the Adult Education Center serves the whole reservation. Therefore, the project offered the potential to attract more local participation.

From the start, the project had immense interest from our own academic community and from the students at Penn State. We received a record number of applications from students, and were approached by several alumni volunteers interested in helping out. We decided to capture the energy generated by this interest and include as many students and volunteers as possible. We ended up with a record number of participants: twenty-thirty students from each school, six faculty members, and five-ten alumni volunteers, making the head count about sixty-five people. Since we had never built a public straw bale building before we had no way of knowing whether or not these were reasonable numbers. We had heard from Red Feather Development Group, however, that there were other projects in the area that could use extra hands, so we decided to give it a try knowing that these could absorb excess volunteer labor if necessary.

This also was the first site for an AIHI straw bale building that engaged an existing architectural fabric. The campus of Chief Dull Knife College is made up of three major buildings around a green lawn and facing a large parking lot. Students decided to locate the new building between the main classroom building and the library; it was pushed back away from the classroom building to create a small plaza between the two. The plaza was envisioned as a place for gathering, while the Adult Education Center building was a place for more private, personal growth and learning.

Placing the building between the two others meant that it would not have the opportunity to capture as much natural light as earlier buildings we'd built on the Plains. Straw bale, with its thick walls and deeply set windows, and a

The Adult Education Center sits between two older college buildings.

The thick, voluminous straw-bale walls contrast the thin aluminum of adjacent college buildings.
Photo by Owen Gump.

size and height regulated by the large modular units of straw bales themselves, does not welcome light in to begin with. To address this issue in the Adult Ed building, students once again pushed the structural system, developing an innovative method of raising the roof above the bale walls to create a clerestory window channel. In addition, they used floor-to-ceiling windows in the front façade of the building, which not only help brighten the entry but also distinguish this building as a public structure as opposed to a private home. An airlock entry allows two layers of floor-to-ceiling windows between interior and exterior, thereby limiting some of the heat loss that large openings would otherwise permit.

The vaulted ceiling and curving interior walls of the building offer the opportunity for nooks where students can read and study. As child care is hard to come by on the reservation, a children's area provides informal daycare for students with young family members, addressing one of the previous barriers to taking advantage of the services provided at the center. Local Northern Cheyenne artists provided artwork for the building in the form of tile mosaics along the curving wall that depict bison migrations across the Plains.

In the course of the project it became apparent that the numbers of people we'd brought were too large and there wasn't enough work to go around. In a fieldwork-based educational program, this is a major problem— if students aren't doing the fieldwork, presumably they aren't learning. We offered them the opportunity to work on other straw-bale projects going up on the reservation to absorb some of the extra hands, and incorporated a cultural research assignment into the curriculum that ended up being highly successful. In the end, however, the program coordinators learned a valuable lesson about the delicate balance that makes the student labor-to-work ratio effective for learning.

Each stone in the courtyard has an important symbolic meaning. Photo by Matthew Ford.

Whether we like it or not, there are a lot of people here who are not literate, who can't read or write beyond a certain level. We have a very strong literacy program here that becomes a transition into adult education. Education allows people to begin to appreciate who they are, to open up and realize for the first time in their life that higher education is something they can accomplish and feel really good about.

The AIHI students had an incredible opportunity to learn as much as they could in two weeks about the culture of the Northern Cheyenne. I see that as a stepping stone to sending some of our students to Penn State or the University of Washington to do the same kind of exchange, to have the opportunity to explore a different culture and see things that they wouldn't see otherwise.

Bill Wertman
Vice President, Chief Dull Knife College

Artist Bentley Spang worked with local Cheyenne high school students to create this courtyard in the found space created by the building's position on the site. Photo by Matthew Ford.

Gardeners work in their personalized plots. Photo by Steve Badanes.

Client: Inter*Im Community Development Association (ICDA)

Funding: Seattle Department of Neighborhoods; Boeing; Safeco Corporation; MacMillan Bloedel; UW Department of Construction Management; Mutual Materials

Budget: 1990: n/a; 1991: n/a; 1996: $12,000

Program: overall garden amenities including gateways, seating, walls, stairs, wash areas, and compost bins; accessible garden terraces, kiosks

Challenges: steep grade on site; communication between students and elderly gardeners

Lesson: simplify construction solutions so work is available to students regardless of experience

The Danny Woo International District Community Garden is a food-producing garden in Seattle's predominantly Asian neighborhood where residents can claim plots and grow vegetables and fruit. The garden is a nationally recognized project spearheaded and managed by the Inter*Im Community Development Association (ICDA) of Seattle. ICDA is a community-based nonprofit organization dedicated to the stabilizing and revitalizing Seattle's International District (ID) neighborhood, while avoiding displacement and gentrification. Throughout its twenty-seven-year history, ICDA's work has focused on community development and advocacy in the ID on behalf of elderly, low-income, and minority residents, and the nurturing of the ID as the cultural focus for the larger Asian Pacific community.

The Danny Woo Garden is made up of more than 100 garden plots on a steeply terraced, south-facing slope overlooking the ID neighborhood and South Main Street. Named after the community activist who donated the land for the garden, it was built through the efforts of countless volunteers. These plots are tended primarily by elderly low-income residents. Most elderly residents of the ID live in tiny apartments or single-occupancy hotel rooms, so the garden provides a cherished opportunity to work the earth. This pastime provides a source of purpose and pride for these elderly people, and, as they get to know the other gardeners, a social network linking them with the larger community. Most of the gardeners are from Asian countries (Korea, China, the Philippines, Taiwan, Vietnam, and Japan) where farming was their way of life; therefore, the garden enables them to continue with traditional, familiar activities and grow herbs and vegetables that link them to their homeland. For the larger ID community, the garden serves as a source of community pride and spirit and as the site of special annual community festivities.

Leslie Morishita, a graduate of the UW Master of Architecture program, first got Professor Badanes and the Neighborhood Studio interested in the Danny Woo Garden. She took on the task of building a tool shed for the garden as an independent-study project with fellow student Brian Reading in 1989. Other students began to turn their attention toward the garden, and soon Professor Badanes was asked to do a design/build studio at the site. In the summer of 1990, the Neighborhood Studio did its first project at Danny Woo and returned in the summer of 1991 to continue the work. These studios gave the students an opportunity to work in a unique cultural and social setting within a city they already knew well. They were encouraged to try to understand the different perspectives of members of this international community, and to accommodate this diversity in their designs.

The steep slope of the donated land called for extensive stairs and retaining walls to make the site navigable. In 1990, however, the garden was still fairly informal, with makeshift staircases and retaining walls and almost no amenities such as signage or gates. During the two consecutive summer studios, the Neighborhood Studio addressed these issues by building an entry gateway, garden kiosks to rest in, vegetable washing areas, seating, and a pig-roasting pit and barbecue area. In addition, several staircases and retaining walls were improved by the students.

The community design process was essential in the design phase of this project. In some cases, feedback helped students further define the program, as with the pig-roasting pit and the bypass wood framing system that recalls traditional Japanese and Chinese wood architecture. More than a superficial nod to historic building methods, this system is easily understood and maintained by volunteers in the community. In addition, it is a good system for student labor because it has higher tolerances and, by not limiting students to precisely cut dimensions, is more forgiving of unskilled work. These early Neighborhood Studio projects helped to make the garden more beautiful and safer, and made the elderly gardeners feel more secure in their claim on this piece of land, which is being increasingly squeezed by the pressures of downtown development.

By spring 1996, however, a new challenge had emerged at the Danny Woo Garden. Some of the garden's advocates at the ICDA began noticing that increasing numbers of long-time elderly gardeners had stopped tending their plots. Climbing the hill to the garden was becoming too difficult, and the numerous steps and idiosyncratic paths improvised from salvaged boards and recycled materials were risky for people for whom a fall could be devastating. Losing the opportunity to garden and care for something living shrinks the world and diminishes the quality of life of these frail elderly. ICDA approached the Neighborhood Studio with the challenge to create a series of accessible gardens for these gardeners at the upper, undeveloped edge of the site, which would be easily accessible from the street above.

The studio designed and built pathways, rails, seating, and raised garden beds that are sensitive to the special needs of the elderly and embrace the unique character of the community garden and the ID. Planting beds are waist high so gardeners don't have to bend over or get down on their knees. Ample railings and ramps make the circulation safe, and the stone and concrete pavers chosen minimize the threat of slipping and falling. This studio provided students with an opportunity to explore elderly design issues within a unique cultural context: in Asian countries, elderly people are the most re-

Photo by Steve Badanes.

The garden plots have views of downtown Seattle and the Olympic Peninsula. Photo courtesy of Inter*Im.

Waist-high plots make gardening easier for elderly gardeners. Photo by Jared Polesky.

A system of ramps gives wheelchair access to the accessible plots from the street above the garden. Photo by Jared Polesky.

spected and revered members within both the family unit and the larger society. Ultimately, students met their own most difficult challenge: to execute this project in a way that would bring dignity to the aging gardeners while avoiding calling attention to their frailty.

The Neighborhood Design/Build Studio's early work at the Danny Woo Community Garden taught the program some valuable lessons about design/build education. It became clear that even complex challenges, such as those presented by this unique site, had to be met with simple solutions. Otherwise, only the most skilled and experienced students would be able to have a hands-on learning experience.

The relationship between the Neighborhood Studio and the Danny Woo Garden has been infinitely beneficial to the curriculum and work of the UW BASIC program. Over the years, it has given students the opportunity to become familiar with the ID as a strong Seattle neighborhood facing challenges and issues that reflect the larger planning, development, and social issues currently confronting low-income communities in Seattle and beyond.

Photo by Steve Badanes.

Client: St. Andrews Housing Group, Inter*Im Community Development Association (ICDA)

Funding: St. Andrews Housing Group; ICDA

Budget: $2,500

Program: gazebo, decks, benches, work areas, and storage facilities

Challenges: long commute to work site; entirely new "planned" community made context hard to evaluate

Lessons: choose projects closer to home; public parks need good management after completion

The Neighborhood Design/Build Studio formed a lasting relationship with the local nonprofit organization ICDA during the three earlier studio projects it did at the Danny Woo Garden. While most of ICDA's work focuses on the International District adjacent to downtown Seattle, it also sponsors housing initiatives for low-income Asian people in adjacent suburbs and other parts of the city. In 1998 ICDA approached Professor Badanes with a project for the Neighborhood Studio: they wanted to build another, smaller community garden at a new housing project in Issaquah, Washington, a suburb about fifteen miles east of Seattle.

Highland Gardens, located within the master-planned community of Klahanie, provides fifty very low-income households with permanent housing in a stable, supportive, multicultural community setting. The project grew directly from a unique community-participation design process within the Lao hill tribe communities of Hmong, Mien, and Kmhmu Southeast Asian refugees. The community, designed by Mike Pyatok, a professor at the CAUP and renowned housing architect, emphasizes comfortable living for large and extended families, and the site layout and amenities support and encourage mutually beneficial relationships. Townhouse units are arranged around shared courtyards, and a community building includes an office, laundry facilities, a community kitchen, and a large meeting/activity room that opens onto a trellised patio/barbecue area. A tot lot and half basketball court are included for the many children that live here. A community garden provides a very important amenity for those immigrants and refugees from agrarian backgrounds, while also offering opportunities for sharing and community-building within the project.

The decision to accept this project was difficult for the Neighborhood Studio faculty simply because it lacked the convenience of earlier urban sites. Students would have to drive a half hour to and from the site at least four days a week. In addition, the previous projects were mostly in nearby Seattle neighborhoods, which made a tight body of work for students, volunteers, and donors to visit and understand. Ultimately, however, it became clear that this housing project offered a great opportunity to build upon things the studio had learned at Danny Woo and assimilate them into a new community that needed identity and resources.

The Neighborhood Studio team designed and built a gazebo, decks, benches, work areas, and storage facilities in the community garden. They also laid out the garden plots and landscaped some of the site. All structures respond to the craftsman-style detailing of the other buildings on the site and are built with a modified bypass wood system similar to that at Danny Woo.

Upon completion, the community garden quickly became a treasured amenity in this award-winning housing project.

However, a later visit to the site showed that the gardens had been poorly managed and maintained. Very few plots seemed to be in use; gardeners hadn't been there to use and protect the pavilion and work areas. Unlike the Danny Woo Garden, which is directly around the corner from the ICDA office in Seattle and has a full-time manager to coordinate the individual gardeners, Highland Gardens is fifteen miles from ICDA and its management falls among the tasks of already-busy ICDA employees. It is apparent that a collective garden like this relies on good management for good participation. Architecture alone cannot create a positive collective experience, though it can support and enable those that are in place. Current ICDA planner Leslie Morishita, the former UW student who built the Danny Woo tool shed, is implementing a management program for the Highland Gardens that is reenergizing the project.

Photo by Jared Polesky.

Students fasten connections on the bypass wood system. Photo by Steve Badanes.

Photo by Jared Polesky.

Pavilion, Gateways, and Footbridge at Bradner Gardens Park
Seattle, Washington
1999–2000

A system of gateways and park furniture establishes clear edges for the park. Photo by Jared Polesky.

Photo by Jared Polesky.

Client: Friends of Bradner Gardens Park; King County Conservation District; King County Master Gardeners; Seattle Department of Parks and Recreation; Seattle P-Patch programs; Seattle Tilth Association; Seattle Tree Stewards

Funding: Seattle Department of Neighborhoods; Puget Sound Urban Resources Partnership

Budget: 1999: $9,000; 2000: $13,000

Program: 1999: garden structures including eastern and southern arbor gateways, benches, bridges, and retaining wall; 2000: central pavilion, western arbor gateway

Challenge: very experienced builders sought challenging design (2000)

Lesson: when the skill level is high, push the quality and details of student design (2000)

Bradner Gardens Park was at one time an underused 1.6-acre open hilltop space in the Mount Baker neighborhood of Seattle, surrounded by single-family residences. In 1971, the city bought it as park land, but for many years it sat relatively unused and was only informally cultivated. It boasts a spectacular view of downtown, and for this reason the former mayor of Seattle, Norm Rice, saw it as an ideal development opportunity for Mount Baker, which had long been one of Seattle's more economically depressed neighborhoods. Residents, however, disagreed. Over the years, personal attachment had formed to the plot of land as local residents had used it for impromptu pea-patch gardens. These residents got together with the King County Conservation District, King County Master Gardeners, Seattle Parks and Recreation, Seattle P-Patch programs, Seattle Tilth Association, and Seattle Tree Stewards and formed the Friends of Bradner Gardens Park. This grassroots organization successfully resisted the development proposals by getting a citywide initiative put on the 1998 ballot that ultimately saved the plot as a neighborhood park. Today the site is home to sixty-one garden plots tended by local residents, as well as extensive demonstration gardens and public open spaces and amenities.

In 1998 Friends of Bradner Gardens Park received a substantial grant from the Seattle Department of Neighborhoods and the Puget Sound Urban Resources Partnership for park improvements, and asked for the Neighborhood Studio's participation. The 1999 Neighborhood Studio's charge was to design and construct elements that would create edges for the park, formalizing its presence in the community. Pea-patch gardens often get lost in the urban landscape because their forms are low and organic, and best understood from above.

Using "Urban Agriculture" as the theme for the project, students designed and built an arbor over the east entry, an arbor and street-retaining wall on the south edge, and a footbridge over a streambed that runs through the site. The arbors on the east and south entries are constructed of cedar supported by gabion columns built from unpainted steel and heavy wire mesh filled with quarry spall. Some of the gabions in the south arbor are reliquaries for old lawnmowers and yard tools. The retaining wall supporting the trellis along this south perimeter is made of recycled sidewalk scraps. At the east gate, cedar benches and a cast-concrete table welcome visitors. The reinforced concrete footbridge is found near the center of this site; it was cast in place and has a low laminated cedar railing. These installments have a strong architectural presence, thanks to the students' adventurous ideas about materials—combining steel, stone, and wood in alternative ways. The students' response to the theme of urban agriculture helped determine the materials palette, as well as the need for durability, longevity, and safety.

The Neighborhood Studio was invited back in spring 2000 to build a central pavilion and west entry arbor for the gardens. This year's studio was filled with experienced builders, and the design solution became very complex. The pavilion has a leaf-shaped roof of cedar skip sheathing covered with site-fabricated Zincalume roofing panels. The large Glu-Lam support beams were fabricated in the central court of Gould Hall at the UW Department of Architecture and trucked to the site for installation on Earth Day 2000.

The west entry arbor mirrors the materials and techniques of the early arbors: steel, wire mesh, stone, and cast-in-place concrete. It features four planter boxes for annual color, trellises for vines, and a wavy bench that faces the children's play area. With the completion of this third gateway, Bradner Gardens Park has distinct boundaries on three of its four sides. The gateways give the gardens an architectural presence, so that the size and layout of the space can be understood upon entry, and the central pavilion gives the gardens a clear center and point of destination.

Over the years, the urban agriculture theme, as defined by the materials used in the initial interventions, has been scrupulously maintained. It has been easy for new elements to follow the language started by the design/build students because the materials are easy to find and use, and the construction process is easy for novices to understand. The Neighborhood Studio program has found that this is essential in community work, which is usually maintained and continued by volunteers; the systems must be accessible to a variety of skill levels and, more importantly, fun to work with.

Photo by Jared Polesky.

Because we were so close to Interstate 90, the site had not developed as a park right away, like the other nineteen or twenty parcels around the city. The lot was vacant for thirty years or more. Finally, a temporary school was built here, with a basketball court and a big grassy field. After thirty years, the plywood backboards of the old basketball court were rotting and dandelions and weeds were coming up through the asphalt, but the kids played there because there wasn't any other nearby facility. Then, in the mid-eighties, when we had a lot of Southeast Asian immigrants coming in, a little pea-patch was put in for them so that they could garden and raise food for their families. That was the original garden on this site, and it created a kind of outdoor community center for the entire neighborhood; more people came to the garden than just the gardeners. It created a bond between neighbors.

Joyce Moty
Gardener, Bradner Gardens Park

The central pavilion's leaf-shaped roof rests gently on concrete columns. Photo by Jared Polesky.

Project Credits

Escuela San Lucas
1995

Steve Badanes, Joel Bakken, Eric Baldwin, Tim Becker, Alexandra Brigard, Richard Brya, Barbara Bussetti, H. Weston Drumheller, Liz Ellis, Alfredo Garcia, David Goldberg, René Mancilla, Anne Vernez Moudon, Timothy Myhr, Sergio Palleroni, Rico Quirondongo, Stephanie Stanfield, Penelope West, Jeffrey Woodward

1996

Cori Anderson, Steve Badanes, David Bamford, Linda Beaumont, Kelley Brooks, Alan Carandang, Greg Carter, Ben Chung, Rachel Conly, Carl Domínguez, Patricia Dunlavey, Lap-Chan Fong, Nah Greenberg, Jeffrey Hegg, Emily Hennings, Pedro Hernández, Eric Hopp, Hans Hundsnurcher, Jonah Ing, Stan Jaworowski, Hisakata Kobayashi, Nora Leininger, René Mancilla, Joshua McNichols, Joanne Olsen, Mark Oltoff, Sergio Palleroni, Jenny Quanrud, Daniel Simons, Amy Strukmeyer, Kim Sykes, Penelope West, Daniel Wickline, Porter Winston, Margaret Wong

1997

Steve Badanes, Linda Beaumont, Mathew Buchanan, John Cashman, Melanie Como, Patrick Doran, Andrés Eulate, Jill Eulate, Jackie Green, Stefan Hampden, Justin Hendrickson, Rebecca Hodgdon, Meng Huang, Hisakata Kobayashi, Gunter Koehnlein, Dean Kralios, Francis Lee, Margarette Leite, René Mancilla, Karen McCaughan, Julie McLendon, Friederike Meyer, Catalina Mojica, Elizabeth Neace, Sheryl Newbold, Jason Oppenheim, Sergio Palleroni, Mary Robins, Daniel Simons, Jennifer Smith, Tony Stefan, Calvin Tam, Rumi Takahashi, Vu Tran, Penelope West, Jessie Whitesides, Kirsten Wild, James Wong

Casa de Salud Malitzin
1998

Steve Badanes, Alicia Collora, Rachel Connolly, Sotirios Chainis, Nina Escher, Sean Fleming, Brian Franey, Jutta Hagemeier, Ryan Harasimowicz, Shawn Harris, Sanjeev Hass, Jeff Hegg, George Hideg, Tommy Hsieh, Nathan Jenkins, Tara Kolff, Bingram Lai, Susan Lee, Rob Lloyd, René Mancilla, Joyce Maund, Karen McCaughan, Catalina Mojica, John Olson, Pam Orzeck, Sergio Palleroni, Betsy Power, Michael Quesenbury, Nereyda Rodríquez, Pam Schaeffer, Ziad Shehab, Erica Shrader, Lynn Smalley, Ian Towler, Allen Tsai, Bill Tsai, Emily Wheeler, Jessie Whitesides, Kurt Wong, Jorge Zambrano

1999

Steve Badanes, Laura Ball, Linda Beaumont, Ruta Bertulis, Rachel Connolly, Nathan Contreras, J. Michael Clifford, Jennifer Dickey, Lindy Ekin, Kevin Eng, Danielle Faris, Vincent Gonzales, Michael Grasley, Jeff Hegg, Andrew Hetlevdt, Jessyca Jones, Andy Koch, Diantha Korzun, Brian Lenz, René Mancilla, Jason Manges, Joshua Masterson, Karen McCaughan, Mr. Ming, Godwin Moy, Rosalie Mullin, Jeffrey Oschner, Alan Paden, Brian Palidar, Sergio Palleroni, Amy Potter, Trudy Powers, Martine Sanders, Ryan Singer, James Slater, Michael Smith, Jeroen Teeuw, Susan Ulep, Scott Petrie Vandever, Tori Williamson, Chad Zettle

Escuela Rosario Castellanos

Jim Adamson, Steve Badanes, Kristin Barrero, Holly Batt, Matthew Bietz, Austin DePree, Carlos Espinosa, Jason Hanner, Todd Hoffman, Stephanie Ingram, Nicole Kistler, Brad Kress, Jason Laer, Jennifer Lau, René Mancilla, Jason Manges, Mark McCarter, Charles McHale, Gretchen McPhee, Sergio Palleroni, Cheryl Sánchez, Eric Shelton, Lisa Sidlauskas, Ming-Lee Yuan, Tori Williamson, Kristin Wall

Urban Organic Agricultural Center & Biblioteca Pública Municipal Juana de Asbaje y Ramírez

Jim Adamson, Chris Armes, Linda Beaumont, Steve Badanes, Holly Batt, Sam Berry, Jeffrey Briggs, Gingi Cabot, Julie Chen, Kerry Coyne, J. Crone, Jason Davis, Renee DelGaudio, Josh Distler, Natalia Echeverri, Jim Garrett, Marn Heggen, Stephanie Ingram, Kirste Johnson, Young Joo Kahng, Sharon Khosla, Japhet Koteen, Erica Leak, Jason Lear, Sally Ann MacGregor, Jason Manges, Oscar Mendoza, Ellen Mirro, Frances Nelson, Alan Paden, Sergio Palleroni, Bruce Parker, Geoff Piper, Jena Restad, Austin Shaw, Tracy Shriver, Jeff Speert, Mathew

Sullivan, Anna Tamura, Kristen Taylor-Foley, Emily Terray, Danielle Wyss, Ken Yocum

U.S. Pavilion
Jim Adamson, Gemma Alexander, Viola Augustin, Steve Badanes, Jim Beckett, Alicia Braman, Laura Carney, Troy Coleman, Mike Denlinger, Tyler Dierks, Maria Do, Morgan Elliot, Lisa Ferrier, Geoff Gay, Kiki Gram, Walter Grey, Jesse Hager, Marn Heggen, Chuck Henry, Stephanie Ingram, Sharon Khosla, Kristen Kildall, Lori Kirsis, Craig Maldonado, Jason Manges, Brice Merriman, Christina Eichbaum Merkelbach, Mark Merkelbach, Anne Morris, Galen Nourjian, Anna O'Connell, Sergio Palleroni, Brian Purdy, Heidi Reinke, Todd Smith, Billy Stauffer, Sean Smuckler, Gretchen Stromberg, Rachael Watland, Willie Welzenbach, Rick Whitworth, Ken Yocum

Unidad Básica de Rehabilitación
Jim Adamson, Steve Badanes, Angela Berry, Jenny Burdzinski, Molly Cherney, Zakaria Chida, Morea Christenson, Kendra Crismier, Kate D'Archangel, Ian Fair, Chris Hawley, Bray Hayden, Chuck Henry, Cassie Hillman, Craig Hollow, Keasa Jones, Ariel Kemp, Devin Kleiner, Dave Knight, Justin Lowe, Laura Malkasian, Jason Manges, Devon Mayhugh, Christina Eichbaum Merkelbach, Mark Merkelbach, Sergio Palleroni, Jenna Rauscher, Casey Rogers, Carolyn Salisbury, Margaret Simon, Peter Spruance, Billy Stauffer, Corinne Thatcher, Cole Thompson, Oscia Timschell-Linville, Megan Tremain, Jennifer Uh, Stephanie Wascha, Meredith Webster, Sandie Woo, Brian Zeallear

Maldonado Farm
Ruta Bertulis, Gloria Day, Marc Einhorn, Carlos Espinosa, Raffaele Exiana, Sora Key, Anthony Lee, Sergio Palleroni, Robert Pellegrini, Galina Shevchenko, Jeffrey Smith

Esperanza
Sara Carlson, Erica Leak, Sergio Palleroni, Penelope West, Mark Wilson

Peggy White House
Min-Jung Cho, Misun Chung, Raffaele Exiana, Michael Grasley, Stephan Hoedemaker, Maureen Intihar, Sora Key, Caroline Kwak, Brian Lenz, Gretchen McPhee, Sergio Palleroni, Marianne Pulfer, David Riley, Mathew Rinka, Jeroen Teeuw

Fast Wolf House
Rick Berliner, Michael Buragas, Gingi Cabot, Brendan Connolly, Jason Davis, Erica Leak, Brian Lenz, Christopher Oh, Sergio Palleroni, Geoff Piper, David Riley, Jaime Scates, Tracy Shriver, Penelope West, Rick Whitworth

Martha Bear Quiver House
Boaz Ashkenazy, Cherie Bulbous, Chan Cheang, Tami Chen, Mike Denlinger, Matthew Garrett, Bray Hayden, Anne

Laughlin, Brian Lenz, Carla Palavecino, Sergio Palleroni, David Riley, Taylor Simpson, Myoungsub Song, Nan-Ching Tai, Andrew Tech, Jeff White

Chief Dull Knife College
Adult Education Center
Angela Berry, Kathelene Bisko, Emily Chaffee, Zakaria Chida, Thomas Ciccarelli, Travis Crum, Kate Frisbie, Tressa Gibbard, Sally Gimbert, Catherine Greenleaf, Grace Heicher, Cassie Hillman, Melissa Kalwanaski, Fulya Kocak, Anne Laughlin, Sara Leland, Brian Lenz, Bethan Llewellyn, Katie Myers, Joshua Nicholson, Carla Palavecino, Sergio Palleroni, Robert Peterson, David Riley, Heidi Reinke, Michael Rí os, Heather Rossi, Christa Scott, Nicolette Slagle, Peter Spruance, Andrew Swartzell, Andrew Tech, Corinne Thatcher, Samantha Wechsler, Emily Whitbeck, Jeffrey White, Scott Wing, Ivy Wong, Sandie Woo, Brian Zeallear, Kristen Zeiber, Lori Zimmaro, Katherine Zimmerman

Danny Woo International District Community Garden 1996
Steve Badanes, Jennifer Caudle, Patricia Dunlavey, Susan Elkan, Huyen Hoang, Michael Mackie, Julia Park, Laila Podra, Damon Smith, Susan Sprague, Jay Thoman, Sylvia Vierthaler, Penelope West, Margaret Wong

Play Courts at the UW Experimental Education Unit 1995
Steve Badanes, Gerald Beltran, Arthur Cole, Craig Compton, Kay Compton,

Gabriel Hajiani, Karen Hovde, Gregory Kewish, Jennifer Paris, Barley Phillips, Xylon Saltzman, Damon Smith, Jon Smith, Tobin Thompson, Audra Tuskes

1997

Steve Badanes, James Baurichter, Scott Carr, John Cashman, Erik Fish, Hans Hansen, Michael Herbst, Young Kim, Kirk MacGowan, Kim Magnussen, Christopher Patterson, Erika Price, Derek Rae, Trevor Schaaf, Damon Smith

Highland Gardens at Klahanie

Steve Badanes, Steve Brown, Ian Butcher, Ken Camarata, Marlene Chen, Sean Fleming, Jay Greening, Mark Jones, Jeffrey Kebschull, Angela Meisner, Douglas Norem, Ronald Pizarro, Damon Smith, Marcus Thomas, Lisa Youk

Bradner Gardens Park

1999

Steve Badanes, Jeffrey Boone, Julie Chen, Sam Chung, Stewart Germain, Chain Jingjang, Julie Matsumoto, Renee Peterson, Ryan Rhodes, Damon Smith, Michael Smith, Daria Supp, Michael Weller

2000

Steve Badanes, Sharla Bear, Todd Biggerman, Chris Countryman, Julie Elledge, Michael Godfried, David Lipe, Trygve Oye, Alexander Pfeiffer, Daniel Poei, Christopher Samujh, Errett Schneider, Damon Smith, Winnie So, Todd Wolf

T. T. Minor Elementary School Performance Stage

2001

Joshua Abbell, Steve Badanes, Erica Burns, Renee Del Gaudio, Jamie Fleming, Jay

Greening, Thea Habersetzer, Lai Ling Kong, Aaron Pleskac, Andres Quintero, John Schack, Damon Smith, Matthew Somerton, Natalie Thomas, Michael Wells, Sara Wilder, Matthew Woodhouse-Kent

2002

Steve Badanes, Jim Beckett, Kari Callahan, Mark Davis, Roy Hague, Ariel Kemp, Collin Kwan, Chen-Yi Lee, Dan Malone, Rene Nishikawa, Brian Purdy, Mike Rausch, Damon Smith, Jonas Weber, Lea Fan Yang, Mei Yee Yap, Daisuke Zaoya

Juan Maria Morelos Elementary School Solar Kitchen

Jim Adamson, Jeff Anderson, Aaron Booy, Kate D'Archangel, Rebecca Dixon, Matthew Eaton, Robert Ernst, Richard Jackman, Jay Johnson, David Kaplan, Dan Karas, Devin Kleiner, Lora Lillard, Matthew Lillard, Mathew Lipps, Jason Manges, Mark Merkelbach, Michael Merkle, Heather Nickel, Sergio Palleroni, Jessica Pennell, Erik Perka, Roman Pohorecki, James Potter, James Ramil, Nicole Romano, Edward Rossier, Greg Shiffler, Michel Spruance, Peter Spruance, Emily Stachurski, Michael Tetzloff, Megan Tremain, Kara Weaver, Ethan Whitesell, Mark Wilson, Jaime Young